Poor Richard's Retirement

Retirement for Everyday Americans

By Aaron Clarey

2017

To the standard of class by which all women should hold themselves to, my grandmother.

Happy 90th birthday!

TABLE OF CONTENTS:

INTRODUCTION

Humankind advances quickest through the discovery and realization of ideas. Be it an invention that obsoletes an entire industry, a new technology that revolutionizes an entire economy, or even a simple line of code that changes an entire program, it is these epiphanic "Ah Ha!" moments that advances society by leaps and bounds as opposed to the incremental progress by mere toil and labor. But while this essay will not replace horses with cars or allow you to Skype with friends in Indonesia, it will revolutionize retirement to such an extent that not only will it render modern retirement planning obsolete, but it will put the ability to successfully retire in nearly every one's hands, even those with no savings at all.

This is achieved not through gimmickry, snake-oil salesmanship, or an unrealistically-rosy manipulation of numbers, but through one of those same "Ah ha" moments that has propelled society to the heights it enjoys today. A philosophical overhaul and rethinking of retirement, what it means, and what role it ultimately plays in life. A simple asking of the question "Is what we're doing working, and is there not a better way to do this?" For I contend, through pulling together previous works, research, and philosophy, there is a vastly easier and superior way to retire and society would benefit enormously from it.

However, for this new retirement system to be successful it requires that exact same philosophical overhaul and rethinking on the part of society. Readers of my previous works may already suspect where this is heading, and their suspicions are right. It is the reprioritizing of your fellow man ahead all other endeavors, desires, and dreams in life. And if you're already familiar with this philosophy and the minimalist principles it entails, I apologize for reviewing covered ground. But whereas minimalism, lifestyle choices, and love for your fellow man are stand-alone principles with merit unto themselves, weaving them together into a succinct, comprehensive, practical, and (above all else) superior retirement strategy will be of benefit to all readers, new and old. Regardless, it will not be through "religiously sacking away an extra $100 per month into our IRA" or whatever band aid fixes that have failed us in the past that will solve people's retirement problems today. The key to this "new retirement" will come from within our ability to reprogram ourselves to know what's truly important in life, thereby fundamentally changing what retirement is and what we need in order to retire.

If we can do this, and get all of society to realize conventional retirement planning is not only dead, but unnecessary, impossible, even damaging, it is my sincere belief all of the free world will be able to enjoy a leap forward on par with the invention of the automobile in terms of financial planning and retirement. It is simply a matter of taking the time to sit, think things through, introspect, and ask ourselves what is most important in life. And when you do, I'm quite confident the lion's share of your financial problems will go away.

CHAPTER 1
THE IMPOSSIBLE DREAM

In the perfect world where:
- June and Ward would stay married,
- Sheriff Griffith and Deputy Fife would show up for their morning cup of coffee, and
- Everybody's dad was Mike Baxter,

Every American would:
- Contribute $400 a month to their IRA,
- Earn their standard 8.0% annual return, and
- In 30 years have $600,000 saved up which would comfortably carry them through 20 years of blissful retirement, after which we'd all die painlessly in our sleep.

Birds would chirp, Tom Brady would win another Super Bowl, and Jennifer Aniston would finally confess her burning love and desire for me. This was how it was supposed to happen. This is how actuaries in the retirement planning industry forecasted it to unfold. This is the way it was supposed to be.

There were just a couple problems.

First, actuaries, statisticians, and other financial planning professionals woefully underestimated the increase in people's life expectancies back in the 1940's and 1950's. Back then the average American lived to 68. Today it's 79. And this underestimation proved costly to American employers. Unexpected pension costs from people's unexpected life expectancies were bankrupting entire industries, entire city and county governments, and is the sole reason for the exodus out of defined *benefit* plans (like pensions) to defined *contribution* plans (like 401k's and IRA's). However, the drawback to conventional retirement planning was not so much failed actuarial forecasts or the demise of pensions, but rather conditioning people to save up under the erroneous assumption they'd die at 70, only to find out they were going to live to 80. This has resulted in a decade-sized shortfall in nearly everyone's retirement planning, forcing people to work past retirement, lest they not outlive their money.

Related is a second variable the original founders of conventional retirement planning failed to predict – slowing economic growth. While life expectancy was increasing, therefore increasing the amount of money one would have to save up for retirement, the engine that would generate the money to fund all these rosy retirements was slowing down - the economy.

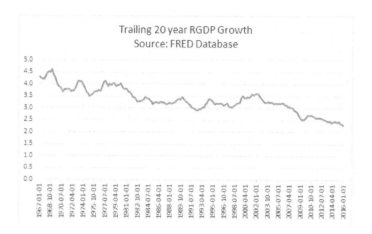

From the 1940's to the 1960's US economic growth averaged around 4.25%. Today the economy only averages 2.2% economic growth. This lack of economic growth also means a lack in wage, income, and salary growth, as well as slower growth in corporate profits, all of which goes to fund these increasing retirement costs. This has resulted in more and more people living paycheck-to-paycheck and rarely, if ever, making a monthly contribution to a retirement plan.

Then there is the issue of stocks and bonds. Why stocks and bonds? Who died and made them the standard investments for retirement? In the olden days people would retire by either selling the farm, living off the family business, or (as was usually the case) work until they died. But in ordaining 401k's, IRA's, 403b's, TSP's, etc., etc., as the primary vehicle by which we save for retirement, the government also unintentionally decreed the stock and bond markets as the only means by which we can retire. This has flooded the market with trillions in retirement dollars, creating the most overvalued stock market in American history except for the Dotcom bubble in the late 90's and the housing bubble in 2007 (and yes, the market is now even more highly valued than the 1929 stock market bubble). These high valuations are all fine and dandy if you happen to be on the cusp of retirement, ready to sell your stocks for a mighty gain. But they prove prohibitively expensive if you are younger and just starting to save for retirement.

And finally, this retirement system was not only designed in different economic times, under different actuarial assumptions, but it was also designed for a completely different group of people. It was designed for the WWII Generation. And to be blunt, we are no Greatest Generation.

Whether you're a Baby Boomer, a Gen X'er, or a Millennial, our generations are laughably inferior to the Greatest Generation. The Greatest Generation went through the Great Depression, fought WWII, produced the largest peace time boom in US history, and as an encore performance won the Cold War. They were frugal, they sacrificed, they did without, they did not spend more than they made, and if they did take on debt it was to maybe buy a house, only to be paid off as quickly as possible. Today's generations just don't compare. We borrow money to lease cars we can't afford, McMansions we'll never be able to pay back, borrow $200,000 to get degrees in "International Relations," with parents who stupidly co-sign on such loans, crippling their own retirements in the process. Even if everybody woke up tomorrow and vowed to be exactly like the Greatest Generation, it's too late as we're too vested in the current system thanks to our bad financial behaviors. Ergo, while modern day financial planning may have been a realistic, mathematically feasible option for the WWII Generation, it does not remain so for the majority of us today.

When you combine all these aforementioned problems, there are three undeniable realities facing us today about modern day retirement.

1. What we're doing isn't working.
2. What we're doing is mathematically impossible.
3. What we're doing is making us miserable.

And if you understand these three realities

and acknowledge what we're doing isn't working, you will realize how vital it is to find a retirement system that actually does. For we can keep going down the road of brow-beating people into socking away money into their IRA's which hasn't worked these past 40 years and will only result in old, impoverished, and miserable people. Or we can come to grips with reality, accurately diagnose the situation, and come up with a new retirement system that will actually work for everyday Americans.

What We're Doing Isn't Working

The simplest and most compelling argument against today's retirement system is that it just isn't working. We can argue all day about what people "should be doing" or what they "shoulda done," but we don't live in "Shoulda Land." We live in the real world. And conventional retirement planning is failing the majority of people.

Statistics vary widely, but of the 75 million Baby Boomers half do not even have a paltry $100,000 in their retirement accounts. Over a third have less than $50,000. And half the Baby Boomers admit they are going to have to work past 65. Only a mere 15% of Baby Boomers have the required standard of $500,000 needed for a successful retirement, and that assumes a lot of rosy assumptions.

It assumes there isn't another stock market crash.
It assumes health care costs don't go up...more than they already have.
It assumes their health maintains itself and they don't incur a ton of medical bills.

And this is for the *MOST MATURE AND RESPONSIBLE GENERATION IN THE U.S. RIGHT NOW.*

When you look at the larger population it only gets worse.

The average retirement savings for your average American was $101,000 in 2013 which is likely around $130,000 now. However, that is the mean average which does not include people with NO retirement savings at all and is also skewed by high net worth savers. When the more-accurate median average is considered, the average American family, *not individual, FAMILY,* has a laughable $5,000 in retirement savings. When you look at families headed up by parents 30 years and under it's an irrelevant $500, a whopping $250 per adult.

However, this assumes you even saved for retirement, of which 36% of American adults haven't. This leaves non-retirement, regular bank savings as hopefully the seed capital or at least a proxy-indicator for the beginnings of would-be future retirement plans. But Americans' bank savings statistics are even worse than their abysmal retirement savings.

In 2015 Google published a quite popular survey which showed 62% of the American adult population only has $1,000 in their savings account. 21% had no savings at all. It meant that should a normal life emergency expense come up, like a car repair or a visit to the hospital, the majority of Americans could not afford to pay it and would have to borrow from family, friends, or a 24% interest-rate-gouging credit card company to make that expense. This is echoed in net worth studies which shows 1/3rd of Americans have no net worth at all, and when student loans are factored in, nearly all college-going-Millennials have a negative net worth. It almost makes planning for retirement a laughable luxury when you can barely afford groceries, rent, or student loan payments and need to borrow money from your mother.

We could go on, but it's painfully obvious Americans simply aren't saving enough for retirement. Admittedly, most of this was self-inflicted - borrowing more than they could pay back, buying things they don't need, partying when they should have been saving, taking on student loans for incomprehensibly stupid degrees. We can enumerate a long list of financial sins. But again, the larger philosophical point is not one of morality or lecturing. It's one of accepting reality. If only 15% of the Baby Boomer generation has managed to successfully retire using today's modern retirement system and...well...*pretty much nobody else,* we must design a retirement system that is conducive to the majority of Americans' economic and financial behaviors, not to mention....

reality.

What We're Doing Is Mathematically Impossible

Assume, for a moment, that magically somehow the entire US population had an epiphany and woke up the next day with the exact same work ethic, fiscal frugality, and financial discipline of the **WWII** Generation. Even if this did happen, relying on the current retirement system would still be mathematically impossible for the majority of people. And the reason is found in the fact we use the stock market as the default investment vehicle to fund our retirements.

As alluded to before, why do we have the stock market (and the mutual funds those individual stocks compose) as the only investment we can make for retirement? Why not selling the farm? Why not living off the family business? What is so special about mutual funds, stocks, bonds, IRA's, 401k's, and 403b's? And the answer is tax deductions.

Without going into the long and boring story of US retirement law, in 1980 a young man named Ted Banna noticed a 1978 provision in the IRS tax code labelled

"401(k)." Though not originally designed to become the default retirement program for the entire US population, he found it could be repurposed by employers to offer an effective retirement plan for their employees, the largest benefit being you could write off your contributions to this new "401k plan." Even though this would cost the government money, providing a financial incentive in the form of a tax deduction for people to save for retirement was not only popular, but also made good financial sense. It would prompt people to sock away funds for a rainy day and lessen people's increasing dependence on social security as their primary source of retirement. And so over the past four decades additional laws were passed creating and officially codifying programs like the 401k, IRA, 403b, etc., as the "official" way to save for retirement.

There was, however, an unintended problem.

The problem was that in dedicating the financial markets AS THE ONLY PLACE to invest for 401k's, IRA's, etc., this retirement plan would only work for the generation already on the cusp of retirement (the WWII Generation at the time) and the generation that would be buying into the financial markets on the ground floor (the Baby Boomers). Any generations after would be buying into an artificially inflated market. Worse, it would be at least 30 years before any new generations would have the jobs and therefore the money to invest in the stock market, giving the stock market more than adequate time to have its price driven up beyond what its profits warranted. This has not only made stocks roughly twice as expensive for young investors (and interest rates on bonds abysmally low) but has introduced an impossible and incredibly dangerous variable into today's retirement planning – perpetual capital gains.

In other words, *STOCKS **ALWAYS HAVE TO GO UP.***

Understand that the entirety of the financial planning and retirement industries rely on the stock and bond markets perpetually "going up" (aka – "capital gains") by an average 8-8.5% per year over the long run. If they don't, then there is not enough growth in people's retirement accounts to attain that magical $500,000 threshold by the time they retire. Worse, retirement planning also assumes you will continue to earn 8-8.5% on that $500,000 even after you retire, otherwise you'll run out of money long before you die. This has put the entire focus of the retirement industry on a *stock's price* and not the **fundamentals that actually drive a stock's value.**

And you see this every day.

If you ask a person why they're investing in a stock or a mutual fund, *99*% of them will say, "Because it will go up in price." But this is neither a complete nor satisfactory answer. *WHY* should those stock prices "go up?" What drives them? They just can't "go up forever." There has to be a reason. And there is.

Profits.

Profits are the **ONLY** real reason stock prices should go up. If profits go up by 5%, then the price of a stock should go up by 5%. If profits go down by 10%, then the price of a stock should go down by 10%. But while well-intentioned as it may have been, the advent of the 401k has changed everybody's focus from the fundamentals of profits to the mere price of the stock. And if we use profits or dividends as a barometer as to what stock prices should be, they have increased at roughly twice the rate profits have grown, making stocks twice as expensive. In other words it is the unconscious behavior of mindlessly making monthly contributions into your 401k or IRA for 30 years that has flooded the market with trillions of retirement dollars that would otherwise not be there. This has not only fundamentally changed why people invest ("because it'll go up") but has made the ENTIRE US (and other countries') retirement systems completely dependent upon irrational, unsupported, and perpetual capital gains/price increases.

An entire retirement system reliant upon forever-increasing stock prices is not only highly prone to bubbles, but it raises a VERY IMPORTANT QUESTION - how much do stocks have to go up by for ALL Americans to retire on? Understand this dispenses with the quaint and outdated notion that profits would have to increase too, because if America ever woke up and started looking at the underlying profits of their stock portfolio the market would be halved tomorrow. But let's just idealistically assume in a world of ponies, flowers, unicorns, and Obamacare, stock prices can go up forever for no reason at all. How much would the stock market have to increase by so we could all successfully retire? And it is here the statistics get downright gloomy, impossible, albeit a bit theoretical.

As it stands today, there is roughly $12.25 trillion in retirement savings in US accounts. One might think this $12 trillion would have to support the retirement of all 320 million Americans, but it only needs to support the 75 million Baby Boomers who are on the cusp of retiring in the short run. Still, this corroborates other statistics mentioned before as $12.25 trillion split 75 million ways is $163,333 each, only a third of the magical $500,000 Boomers need to successfully retire today. Relying on the magical "Forever-Increasing-Stock-Market-for-No-Particular-Reason-at-All" that would imply stock (and bond) prices would have to go up 306%...*tomorrow*... for just the AVERAGE

Boomer to retire. Not only is this extremely unlikely, but keep in mind this is on top of the stock market growing at twice the rate it normally should have since 1980. In short, it's mathematically impossible for the stock market to grow enough to adequately pay for one generation, let alone three.

Gen X's prospects for an adequate retirement doesn't fare much better, but they do have hope in that Gen X at least has some time to work with before they reach retirement age. Gen X also boasts an average of $69,000 in retirement savings (though this statistic seems optimistically dubious). Still, assuming the traditional 8% rate of return, 2.5% inflation, and 25 years before Gen Xers retire, that $69,000 nest egg can grow to account for half the required $930,000 ($500,000 adjusted for 25 years of inflation) they would need to retire. But even with this edge, to save the remaining retirement funds would require *every* Gen Xer to contribute $500 *every* month for each and *every* of the next 25 years...which, frankly, just isn't going to happen.

Forget that the $69,000 average is optimistic and by definition means 50% of Gen Xer's have less than that. Also forget that $69,000 is largely due to the stock market tripling since 2009, a performance of which is unlikely to repeat into the future. Gen X has historically lacked the fiscal discipline, and therefore the disposable income, to religiously adhere to such an investment regimen. Furthermore, Gen X'ers are in the thick of having kids, the expense of which will make religious IRA and 401k contributions impossible. Using more realistic assumptions, I estimate the stock and bond markets would have to grow by 14% per year for Gen X to fully retire. A rate of return that is just not going to happen.

And then there's the Millennials.

The Millennial generation brings in an entirely new mathematical impossibility to today's already mathematically impossible retirement system – progressive credentialism. In the 1960's a Baby Boomer could graduate from high school, find a job, and earn enough in a couple years to afford a car, a house, and even a family. But today an educational arms race is in full force as employers demand ever-increasing levels of education for increasingly petty and low-paying entry level jobs.

Want a job?
You need a degree.

You really want the job?
Well, "masters preferred."

And did you get the job?
Sorry, you need to continue with CPE and "continuing education."

And so instead of having the luxury of graduating from high school at the age of 18 and then IMMEDIATELY being able to go to work and start saving for retirement, we've essentially forced Millennials to stay in school for 10 additional and unnecessary years, only to work jobs that, unlike their 1960's counterparts, can barely support the individual, let alone a family.

Unfortunately, this 10 lost years of labor is only half the story in that we've saddled Millennials with trillions of dollars in student loans for those unnecessary degrees we demanded they get. So not only have Millennials lost out on 10 years of work and production that would have gone towards retirement, we've crippled their financial futures for at least the next decade meaning they won't be able to effectively save for retirement until they dig themselves out of their student debt hole around the age of 38.

The financial projections for Millennials are impossible no matter which way you slice it. Starting with nothing at the age of 38 and assuming they have 30 years before they retire, Millennials will either have to fervently contribute $900 a month for each and every one of those 360 months hoping the financial markets maintain their magical 8% increase per year, or they contribute a more realistic $500 a month, but pray to the Gods of Magical Price Increases that the financial markets maintain a porn-star-like performance of 11% per annum for the next 30 years.

Which again, bar a hyper-inflationary environment, just isn't going to happen.

What We're Doing is Making Us Miserable

Retirement planning is just one piece of our overall personal finance puzzle. And while people may think retirement is separate from our daily budget, far off in the distant future when we turn 65, the truth is it is directly affected and ultimately determined by the financial decisions we make today. Because of this we need to ask ourselves what are we doing with our personal finances today? How are we leading our financial lives? And what are the consequences not only for the here and now, but our future retirements as well? But perhaps the most important question of them all is one that puts retirement into the ultimate context...

Why do we retire?

Common sense would suggest we retire because we do not like to work. Not that work is evil or that somehow we all hate our jobs, but that we'd much prefer our free time, doing what we like, than work. This, by necessity, makes "work" the opposite of "freedom" in that we are not in charge of our own time while laboring under the employ of our employer. Ergo, the whole point of retirement is to suffer this necessary evil of work so we not only can support ourselves, but also squirrel away some extra funds so that we may retire from it, granting us the freedom to spend our time as we see fit. This concept of work being the antithesis of freedom is so engrained in our psychology that perhaps the holy grail of western civilization is "early retirement," maybe only to be trumped by "making it rich."

But the irony is that if we take a clinical and unbiased look at our financial behaviors today we do anything but work to be free. Matter of fact nearly all of our financial decisions enslave us to work forever. And it is in losing sight of the real point and purpose of retirement that is causing us to be miserable today.

Take for example how we lived life in 1955 versus how we live life today. In 1955 the average household of 3.5 persons managed to live, just fine, off of a $25,000 salary (adjusted for inflation). They may not have had flat screen TV's or cell phones, but they successfully got by on less than half of the $56,000 median household income we do today. Further speaking to work versus freedom, the families of the 50's did so on one income, typically the father's. This didn't mean the mother didn't work (child rearing, housekeeping, budgeting/shopping, etc., was certainly a real job), but it meant less of the parents' cumulative time was spent at work and away from their family. It also beget a whole host of benefits such as properly reared children, a well-maintained home, and familial stability. I know we all like to mock and ridicule June and Ward, but they never got divorced and Jerry and The Beaver weren't in the psychologist's office every week after being moved like a chess piece between daycare and their recently divorced parents' homes. Finally, the magic of the 1950's family budget didn't end there because it managed to support 3.5 people compared with today's budget that, though twice as large, only supports 2.5. In other words, on an inflation-adjusted, per capita basis we spend $22,400 per person today whereas our 1950's counterparts got by on a third of that with $7,100.

So how did they do this?

Simple, they did without.

Though there has been many changes to the economy and American family since 1955, there are two major items that have accounted for the lion's share of the American family budget – housing and transportation. And when we look at these two variables you can see where all this extra money and time is going.

In 1955 the average size of an American house was 983 square feet, contrasted to today's average of 2,700 square feet. It doesn't take a genius to figure out that houses that are THREE TIMES as large will cost more, even when we account for inflation and advances in home construction technology. Worse, however, a house is no longer merely a place to eat, sleep, and raise a family. Americans today demand their houses have all these amenities:

a three car garage,
granite countertops,
a pool,
separate bathrooms and bedrooms for each person (anybody remember bunk beds?),
a helicopter pad,
ALL of which "must be in a good school district."

Insisting a house have all these requirements has driven the inflation-adjusted cost per square foot from $73 in 1955 to $104 today, in spite of cheaper construction technology. So even though today we have twice the budget and one full person less to support, we spend 33% of our budget on housing versus 22% what they did in 1955.

The second major budget item is transportation. In the 1950's the average family only had one car. Today we have 2.3 cars per household. However, it is not as simple as saying today we spend 2.3 times as much on transportation. Cars today can last 200,000 miles whereas cars of yesteryear would maybe last 70,000. Cars today are much more advanced both in terms of amenities and safety, whereas cars of the 50's (though beautiful) were not as advanced. And cars are much more fuel efficient than they were in 1955, getting roughly twice the mileage they did 60 years ago. However, the real issue about cars is not so much comparing what we spend today versus what we did in the 50's (as it would be comparing apples to oranges), but how much we should be spending today on *transportation*.

If we are to be completely honest with ourselves we do not buy *transportation* in 2017. We buy *vanity, prestige, and status* that cars falsely confer upon us. And we can't even say we "buy" it as 88% of people lease or finance their ~~vanity~~ cars. Regardless, transportation is truly a secondary consideration. But if we really wanted to, we can easily calculate what it would cost to afford mere transportation in 2017 and not vanity.

33.4 cents per mile.

33.4 cents per mile is the price you would pay per mile assuming you bought a perfectly good used car for $5,000, drove it for 100,000 miles, paid for regular maintenance and upkeep, and didn't have to spend so much on insurance because you're driving a used car, not a brand new Mercedes. This contrasts with 58 cents a mile the IRS uses as an estimate to reimburse people for travel costs which implies we are paying 42% more for vanity and not transportation. If we apply these savings to the $9,500 American households spend per year on transportation today, we would save $4,000 each year, an amount that would fund 2/3^{rds} the average person's retirement.

Ergo, if Americans really wanted to retire, cutting these two expenses alone (housing and transportation) would suffice for the majority of people. But we don't. And the reason we don't is because these two items are an indicator of something more endemic among the American population – overspending. And it is this behavior that is the source of nearly all our misery.
Be it...

buying designer clothes you don't need and that will be out of fashion next year,
buying the latest video game or iPhone the day it comes out instead of waiting six months for it to go on sale by 75%,
eating out at restaurants because you're too busy to cook a meal at home,
drinking at the bar when a bottle at home will suffice for 1/10th the cost,

buying a snowmobile, motorcycle, kayak,
mountain bike or some other expensive toy
you'll never use,
getting a worthless degree at an overpriced
liberal arts college, or
the manicures, pedicures, massages, spa
treatments and facials that do nothing to
fund your IRA,

nearly every item in the average American's
budget has fat that can be drastically cut.
But we don't cut it because we either lack
the self-control to limit our consumption,
don't think about how these things cost us
our retirement in the future, or falsely
believe this materialism will provide us
happiness. Unfortunately, this materialism
comes at a cost beyond the mere price tag of
these meaningless things – our lives and our
happiness. And it does so by costing the
American family their free time, primarily in
requiring a two-income household.

To afford all this unnecessary stuff you now

need what has become a staple of American finances - the two-income family. Most people may glibly accept this concept or think it's the "new normal," but requiring two incomes to support one family sets forth a chain of events that not only undermines the family, but incurs an incalculable toll in terms of time, psychological stress, emotional pain, happiness, and money on the part of all family members.

First, work sucks. For a lucky few it doesn't, but for the remaining 99.8% of us work sucks. It's tiring, it's draining, it's boring, it's exhausting, and it is a mental tax we endure to get a paycheck. It's already bad one person in a household has to do it, but when both have to do it, there is no one at home to play the supportive, rejuvenating, reparative role. Both people suffer, both people are mentally taxed, and both come home stressed with nobody to counter this imbalance. This doesn't necessarily lead to the end of the world, but it does lead to an overly stressed family life and overly stressed family.

The wife snips at the husband, the husband yells at the kids, the kids fight with each other. All of these things are normal in a healthily functioning family, but not at the level, intensity and frequency of two-income households. Having a parent stay at home to be the anchor of the family pays invaluable financial, mental, and psychological dividends, but is forfeited when you place material things above your family's mental well-being.

Second, with work comes a commute. If working as a cubicle slave for an insufferable boss wasn't enough, you get to look forward to a daily, traffic-jammed commute both to and from work. And it only gets better as commutes are getting worse every year, consuming 52 minutes a day for the average American commuter. Prorated over the course of a year this is 208 hours, or 26

FULL WORKING DAYS you spent stuck in traffic and NOT with your family. Double that now because you "need" a two-income family to afford all that "stuff," and that's 52 days both parents aren't spending with their kids or each other. But perhaps the worst way to look at this is what percent of your waking hour free time (non-work, non-sleep time) is wasted commuting. Assuming a nine hour work day, eight hours a sleep a night, and a token amount of chore time, you are easily spending AT LEAST 12.5% of your ENTIRE LIFE'S FREE TIME looking at somebody else's bumper sticker. But hey, at least your wife has LuLuLemon yoga jeans and your kids each have the new iPhone 873.

Third, this all optimistically assumes your children have cars, are of driving age, or are biking to all their various pre and post school activities. And we all know it's more important your kids go to baseball practice, gym practice, hockey practice, theater practice, school newspaper, cheerleading camp, band camp, and the junior high chess club than sit at home with the family for dinner. This means the moment both you and your spouse get home after your exhausting commutes you get to hop right back in that car again and play chauffer to your children. Never mind they too endured their own "work day" at school, and are probably as exhausted as you. It's more important to the family's happiness and integrity that you get them engaged in activities, 24-7, so they socialize with other children properly, win plastic trophies, and maybe win a scholarship for flipping over beams really well or throwing orange spheres through red rings. Everybody comes home around 9PM, thoroughly on edge, mentally taxed, fully-prepared to go to sleep, only to...

do it all over again...

day after day after day....

until the youngest leaves the house...

in 12 years...

at which time you will never have the chance
to spend time with your children during
their childhood ever again. But at least you
drove a leased 7 series BMW to work.

Fourth, having children in pre and post
school activities assumes they are of the age
where they don't need constant adult
supervision. If you have an infant, a toddler,
or just some little tyke who can't be left
alone, either you or your spouse has to stay
home to rear the child. Thankfully, there's
daycare where you can outsource the rearing
and upbringing of your child while you
pursue your all-important career to afford
that all-important stuff.

There is, however, some bad news about
daycare.

With the median American household income of $71,000, that implies a take home pay of $56,800. Split two ways that means each spouse brings home $28,400. Average daycare costs $12,000 per child in the United States and if you have the (roughly) American average of 2.0 children per couple, that means that second income with both spouses working only really nets $4,400.

Understand this and understand this clearly.

Most two-income families are:
- Outsourcing the upbringing of their own children
- To complete strangers
- Passing up on seeing their children grow up
- So BOTH parents can work jobs they don't like
- While suffering commutes that keep them from their families
- AND stressing themselves out in the process

all for an additional $4,400...which would presumably go to buy that all-important stuff. It is truly sad most Americans value stuff more than their spouses, their families, their children's childhoods, or their own free time.

When you tally it all up, this is why Americans are miserable. This is why the majority of Americans cannot afford retirement. It is because we are owned by the stuff we buy. We engage in the rat race, pursuing pointless educations, for taxing careers, life-wasting commutes, just to buy stuff, pointless material things, while abandoning anything and anybody that really matters in life. It's the cause of the majority of divorces in the country, the majority of unvisited parents in nursing homes, and is ultimately responsible for all the country's financial problems. And to throw the burden of saving for retirement on top of Americans' inability to just keep it together, only makes an already-miserable situation impossible to bear.

But this can all end tomorrow.

If we can get rid of our desire for "stuff" the whole rotten system will come collapsing down on itself. Not only will this free us from our slavemasters of materialism, it will do wonders for the American family, their finances, their happiness, not to mention, make retirement a very real possibility for all Americans. It could also (in theory) usher in a new American golden age with higher economic growth, lower debts, accelerated advancements in technology, and a simply better-off society. The only problem is overcoming the innate, genetic addiction Americans have to consumption and materialism.

This is easier said than done because human addiction to consumption isn't a choice, it truly is genetic. Consumption is what has kept us humans alive these past two million years, and merely rereading the above paragraphs won't undo that darwinistic programming. It's literally the same challenge as putting an entire bowl of food in front of a dog and training it not to overeat. It simply isn't in its nature. Therefore, we need a revolutionary line of code that will fundamentally change our psychological programming so that our frontal lobes can override our caveman brains. A catalyst, that when we fully understand and incorporate it into our thinking, will make abandoning materialism not a mentally painful challenge like dieting, but rather a clear and easy choice that we will willingly make. And thankfully one such catalyst exists. It's all around us. It's in ample supply. And best of all this solution to all our financial problems is free!

That catalyst is your fellow man.

CHAPTER 2
YOUR FELLOW MAN

"A truly rich man can afford everything in a mall, but walks out with nothing."
-Unknown

There are two sides to every person's retirement plan.

How much you spend and how much you save.

The problem, however, is today's conventional retirement planning solely focuses on how much you save and gives practically no consideration to how much you spend. This is problematic because, in the end, you truly do not control how much you save. Yes, you control how much you contribute monthly or annually to a 401k. Yes, you can run precise calculations as to how much you'll likely need for retirement. And yes, you can religiously, perhaps even zealously contribute more than is required to err on the side of caution. But because conventional retirement planning relies disproportionately on stock market growth to provide for the majority of your retirement funds, the saving side of the retirement equation is ultimately out of your control. The stock market could crash, hyper-inflation could set in, the government could confiscate your 401k. An infinite number of things, completely outside of your control, can happen rendering the best of retirement planning moot.

Ergo, the entire retirement planning system is disproportionately based on "hope." Hope that the stock market will continue to perform well into the future. And any successful individual will tell you they don't leave their success up to things like "hope" or "luck," but rather actions that are under their control. So whereas you do not control the stock market, and thus how much you will ultimately save, you do, however, control *to the penny* how much you spend. This puts the onus of retirement not on savings, but spending, and I contend this focus is the future of retirement planning.

However, as discussed in the previous chapter, this is easier said than done. Your entire Darwinistic code, your entire genetic programming has you hard wired to consume as much stuff as possible for survival. We can sit here all day, logically, academically, and consciously agreeing with our frontal cortex that, yes, we should all spend less. But like dieting, drugs, alcohol or any other addiction, it is our instincts and basal desires that will win in the end.

This necessitates swapping out or bypassing Americans' addiction to materialism with a superior substitute, the vehicle of which I argue is a love and appreciation for your fellow man. But how do you make humans more entertaining, more desirous, and preferable to the unlimited and infinite amount of material goods and riches this world offers? How does your annoying brother, nagging wife, or neighbor down the street beat a free Ferrari, a lifetime supply of Glenlivet, or winning the lottery? It comes first with understanding why humans are the most important things on the planet. And this epiphany is followed by going well beyond a mere conscious acknowledgement of it, thoroughly and forcibly incorporating it into our psyche. It is at that point our genetic addiction to materialism will have hopefully been overridden and replaced, eliminating the need for material consumption. This in turn directly and drastically affects the spending side of the retirement equation, also directly and drastically lowering the amount we need to save for retirement. In theory, this would lower the traditional required retirement funds from $500,000 to $300,000, while at the same time making it easier to save that $300,000, bringing retirement into the reach of nearly every person in the western world.

It's all feasible and it can happen all tomorrow, but it all hinges on one thing.

Putting humans first in our lives.

The Case for Humans

The politically correct and socially acceptable stance on humans is that all of human life is precious. In the movies you always have to go back to rescue the lost exploration team from the aliens. Political activists always claim "if it just saves one life" then we should spend another trillion dollars on some ungodly program or another. Parents always claim to dearly love their children, and the majority of spouses put on the veneer that they are in eternal, blissful love with one another.

But deep down inside we all know better.

There's seven billion people on the planet, and we don't know, let alone care about the vast majority of them. Most of the humans we do know in our lives we don't like anyway, including everything from bosses, co-workers, fellow commuters, peers, students, teachers, professors, baristas, waiters, waitresses, and that cop that gave you that ticket. And then there's people we outright hate and loathe with the passion of a thousand burning suns. Murderers, criminals, terrorists, politicians, ex's, people who drive slow in the left lane, social justice warriors, and hipsters. Matter of fact, if you think about it, humans are in some regards the worst things on the planet. They commit all crimes, they are the only things on the planet that can hurt us emotionally, they are the cause of all wars, and truthfully, outside natural disasters and disease, they are the cause of all the world's problems.

Even the best humans, the ones we presumably value and cherish the most in our lives, wear thin, compelling an "official stance" on our fellow man that is somewhat forced.

"Employees are our best asset!" (right before the company lays them all off).
"I love my children!" (though I've often thought of drowning them in the river).
"I love my wife!" (with gnashing, grinding teeth).

So if humans are so awful, why then should we like them, let alone make them the whole purpose of our entire existence?

Because humans are infinite.

For all their drawbacks, humans have one thing that nothing else on the planet has, and that is they are infinite. Not in the sense of immortality or they somehow will last forever, but in the sense that they aren't limited, finite, inanimate objects incapable of thought or interaction. Humans are dynamic, constantly-changing, constantly-evolving, intelligent, sentient entities.

Because of this humans are the only thing on the planet that can interact, engage with, and ultimately provide meaning and value to other humans. Your Ferrari, fancy as it may be, is still only a piece of metal and plastic that provides no feedback, response, or reaction to you. Your souped up gaming computer, no matter how advanced the graphics card, is not capable of intelligence, cannot have a conversation with you, and is only capable of interacting with you to the extent other humans have programmed it to. And your McMansion in the suburbs, no matter how much it makes the Jones envious, still cannot debate you, argue with you, contest you, or agree. The most opulent, advanced, and nicest things in the world still cannot hold a candle to a simple conversation with that mere middle-aged man sitting at the bar with his whiskey.

These unique traits of intelligence, infiniteness, reaction, and dynamism further give humans their ultimate value - they are the only thing you can form a relationship with. You can't fall in love with your Ferrari. You can't fall in love with a super computer. And you can't form a friendship with you iPhone 973. They simply aren't capable of interacting with you, challenging you, and loving you back. Not that you would think a physical object is capable of love, but imagine enjoying these things without humans.

Driving a sports car by yourself
Attending a movie by yourself
Playing video games by yourself.
Having a dinner by yourself.
Going on vacation by yourself.

You'll quickly find out it is not the actual things you enjoy, but having the people around you to enjoy them with. And you will also soon find out it is the highest order

of compliment, perhaps the ultimate
measure of your worth as a human being,
when people consciously choose to spend
some of their dwindling, finite time on this
planet with you.

Finally, if none of this convinces you, or
perhaps you consciously agree with it, but
you just don't feel it in your gut, consider
the instance when humans are removed from
your life – a funeral. Funerals provide even
the most cold-hearted, misanthropic of
people a clear, albeit brief insight into what
is most important in life. And the guttural,
visceral reality of a human's value becomes
painfully clear. If you crash your car, lose
your phone, or break a vase, you might get
angry, perturbed at the cost and
inconvenience of replacing such things. But
you do not cry, mourn, and suffer like you
do when a loved one dies. You do not feel
sick to your stomach for days after. And
you don't get clinically depressed. This
alone is proof, whether you consciously

realize it or not, that humans are more
important to us than things.

However, I contend there is much more
happening when there's a death of a loved
one, the insights of which only further
reinforce the importance of humans. For
while it makes complete sense to mourn over
the death of somebody you care about, I
theorize the majority of the mourning is not
because the person died, but because you
failed to spend time with them while they
were alive. And not only do you regret the
decision, but a large part of the mourning is
slowly coming to grips with the fact there
no longer is any opportunity to do so. That
person, that loved one, that engaging,
infinite, dynamic, intellectual being whose
sentience and personality you loved
(romantically or as a brother), has ended
permanently. And there is no way (bar
various religious beliefs) you will ever enjoy
that person again. It only hurts more when
you consider all the time you spent paying

for BMW leases, granite countertops, worthless liberal arts degrees, designer clothes, and other worthless stuff instead of spending time with them.

But hey, you know what? At least you'll have fond memories of that leased Range Rover.

Regardless, it shouldn't take a funeral to shake us out of our rat race haze to cherish the people we love in our life. Worse, waiting until someone dies to appreciate them is not only both stupid and tragic, but impossible since you can't appreciate them when they're dead. And while the point of this essay is to make retirement feasible for everybody through love for your fellow man, perhaps a more important lesson is love for your fellow man itself.

Psychological Adaptation

In theory, the case for humans should be so

compelling that it would naturally and immediately replace our desire for material goods and consumption. Demand for mere material things would dry up, people would pare down their budgets, and a whole new world of financial frugality and freedom would be ushered in tomorrow. The problem, however, is that no matter how compelling the case for putting your fellow man at the center of your life, we still have to overcome hardwired, psychological, genetic, and Darwinistic forces that have been at work on the human brain for the past two million years. Forces that were put there for good reason as they were not only what kept us alive, but were the source of our happiness and meaning. For while materialism and the over-consumption of things are the root cause of most people's financial problems today, they were precisely what kept humans alive...and the species perpetuated...in the past.

These forces present a paradox. It pits our

genetic hardwiring and "hind brain" instincts for survival and happiness in direct opposition to what our conscious, frontal cortex logically knows to be true today. Unfortunately, the frontal cortex only accounts for 25% of the brain's mass and must override the entrenched, engrained, stubborn, and *thrice larger* hind brain. So to overcome this huge psychological disparity is indeed a challenge. However, humans are not completely helpless when it comes to keeping their caveman urges in check. The frontal lobe does exist and has done a pretty good job of preventing us from killing one another in fits of caveman rage. But we also understand what the source of our obsession with materialism is and have even developed ways to treat it – addiction.

Addiction is usually discussed in the context of drugs, booze, and other controlled substances. A person is addicted to heroin. A person is addicted to booze. A person is addicted to cocaine. And heaven help you if you're addicted to meth. But addiction is not relegated to the mere traditional sources of vice and narcotics most people usually associate addiction with. People can also become addicted to sex, addicted to food, they can even become addicted to video games. Ergo, because of the breadth and variety of things people can become addicted to, there is an underlining common thread to addiction. And that common thread is dopamine.

Without going into a long and boring lecture about neurochemistry, dopamine is (one of many) chemicals released into the brain that not only makes you feel good, but increases and intensifies memory so you remember not just the feeling, but what you were doing at that time. This becomes very useful when it comes to survival. If you find some edible berries or use a new technique to slay a saber tooth tiger, dopamine is released in your system not just to give you warm fuzzies, but so you remember what similar environment to find those berries in and what that genius technique was that you used to slay the saber tooth tiger.

Dopamine is also released, curiously, while having sex. These things are not coincidental or unrelated in that all of them help humans survive and propagate the species. Finding new food sources helps keep current humans alive. Learning how to efficiently slay hungry saber tooth tigers definitely helps keeps humans alive. And wanting to copulate helps bring about future humans...who would also presumably like to eat berries, slay saber tooth tigers, and stay alive. All these vital skills are learned and reinforced through the positive reinforcement feelings that dopamine give us. Therefore, all humans, in a sense, are addicted to dopamine because our survival depended on it.

But we are at an incredibly interesting and curious time in the grand scheme of human history, especially as it pertains to our relationship with dopamine.

One, technology has advanced to the point that we can now make synthetic drugs that give us dopamine highs 10 times stronger than slaying the largest of saber tooth tigers ever could. Be it alcohol, heroin, ecstasy, or morphine, one only needs to pop a pill or shoot up with heroin and they'll experience a dopamine rush nobody before 1,000 BC ever did, all for an infinitesimal fraction of the effort. This provides humans with a short cut to get that dopamine fix their entire genetic code has been programmed to chase, but without the productive, life-extending efforts that were required to get it.

Two, while celebrity overdoses, cartels, and drug wars may make headlines because they're sexy, there is another evolution occurring that has brought about addictions that have nothing to do with synthetic substances, but can still bring about those same quick, effortless highs our brains are programmed to seek. Economic growth.

Economic growth is largely considered a good thing, and it is. But an unintentional side effect is that with economic growth, technological advances, and especially advances in agriculture, things that were predominantly scarce in the past, yet vital for our survival, now flow with overabundance.

Food
Water
Clothing
Housing
Heat

And none of this addresses completely new things that were invented since the industrial revolution that also now flow in overabundance.

Transportation, cars, trains, planes, boats.
Media, movies, the internet, music, concerts.
Computers, flat screen TV's, video games,
cell phones.
Chocolates, ice cream, cake, cupcakes, and
those awesome candy diamond rings you can
get at the gas station.

But when you put this into perspective, these
things have only really been around for 200
years. And the economic ability to purchase
them in overabundance for at most 100.
Which, when you compare it to the two
million years the human brain has been
evolving, is nothing. In other words,
technology and the economy are growing
MUCH faster than our brains can evolve
and adapt. So when you have the nearly
limitless amount of material goods this
world has to offer, and the economic means
by which to consume them well beyond
what is necessary for survival, a human brain
that is stuck in 500,000 B.C. survival mode
is going to do what every dog does when

you leave food around.

Consume until he pukes.

Just like your dog's hind brain is unaware of the lavish, posh, opulent lifestyle it has compared to his prehistoric wolf forefathers, so too are our human brains. It is why we buy things we don't need, it is why we eat more than is necessary, and is evidenced in the real world by the increasing amount of credit card debt and obesity rates, especially among Americans. The problem is we no longer live in 500,000 B.C. Our environment has changed rapidly and dramatically. And while the dopamine-led survival strategy served us well for the past 1,999,900 years, today at best it's obsolete, at worst it is hurting us.

The issue is how do you get rid of two million years-worth of genetic conditioning? And, thankfully, we have the answer. For the root cause as to why we consume more than we need/can afford is identical to why alcoholics drink, drug users use, and shopaholics shop – addiction. And while there are tomes of research written about treating addiction and its complex underlying psychology, the solution all boils down to one simple thing.

Detox.

Detox

Of course, "detox" is not so simple. If you talk to anybody who has been a drug addict, an alcoholic, and has gone to rehab they will tell you it is the hardest thing they ever did. And before you look condescendingly upon alcoholics and drug addicts, ask yourself how successful you were in losing that weight you wanted, adhering to that family budget, or giving up smoking. The reality is that we all know consciously, academically, and literally how to end addiction. Simply stop. But we are fighting against a genetically hardwired system that has kept humans alive for millennia of millennia. Still, this doesn't mean we don't have the tools and knowledge by which to end addiction. And since its root cause is dopamine (whether it's meth, sex, food, or spending) we can borrow from conventional addiction treatment techniques to ultimately solve our retirement problems.

It is here we have a wide array of options when it comes to treating addiction. There are 12 step programs such as Alcoholics Anonymous and Narcotics Anonymous. Variants of these 12 step programs such as the SMART Recovery program. Medication wherein a substitute drug is used to supplant the one you're addicted to (much like we are aiming to replace material things with humans). Counseling and therapy with either a support group and/or a therapist. You can enter rehab. And then there's good ole fashioned quitting cold turkey.

But while we have many options to fight addiction at our disposal, not all of them would be ideal to curb spending. For example taking drugs or committing yourself to rehab to adhere to a simple family budget may be a "touch" extreme. Furthermore, the majority of addiction treatments are intended for substance abusers, not chronic shopaholics. i.e. – an entire infrastructure and support system is in place to help alcoholics and drug addicts, but bar some psychologists who specialize in spending addiction, there is no global support network of "Shopaholics Anonymous." This largely relegates our treatment options to those that are within our own control and do not require a pre-established community or support infrastructure. And the treatment that most closely resembles this is one of dieting.

This is no coincidence since that is precisely what you are doing. You are going on a diet. However instead of giving up calories,

fat, carbs and food, you're giving up dollars.
But just like all addictions, this financial diet
hinges on the first (and technically only)
step required to be successful - you quit. No
matter what the technique, no matter what
the treatment, every method of ending
addiction requires you give up your vice. It
is accepting this in your frontal cortex as an
unavoidable law, an unavoidable
consequence, and committing to it that
ultimately determines whether you will be
successful or not. Yes, supplement drugs can
help. Yes going to group therapy sessions
will make it easier. But in the end you will
only succeed when you quit.

Still, being no stranger to vice, alcoholism,
and French silk pie myself, I am very aware
of how exclusively frontal cortex that
thinking is. And while this entire chapter
has been dedicated towards undermining the
genetic and biological addiction we have to
consumption, here are a couple tricks I've
found that help stick to a diet, be it one of

food or finances.

Cold Turkey – Whether addicts realize it or not, you *ARE* going to quit cold turkey. You can entertain that lingering thought that you'll ease off your addiction, having a cheat day here, allowing yourself a spending binge there, but in the end to be successful at breaking your habits, *never using again* is the definition of success. Since this is the unavoidable goal of ending addiction, and is what you're going to HAVE TO DO anyway, there's no reason to fight it, so you might as well just commit to quitting cold turkey. Take your credit cards, cut them up, and strap yourself in for a new financial life.

Just Accept It – Another technique I've found useful is to simply make it a principle in your mind that you aren't going to spend money unless you absolutely have to. This allows you to avoid the debates that well up inside when your hind brain constantly assails your frontal lobes to have another drink, take another hit, have another cookie, or buy another thing. Having a conscious, active, and vigilant adherence to a policy of simply not spending money you don't have to immediately cuts off any chance the hind brain has to lodge an argument, tempting you to go back to your materialism vice.

Time to Mentally Adapt – While the first few days of going on a diet are the hardest, in time your brain adapts to the "new normal." Soon your cravings ebb and the temptation of sweets, booze, and consumerism goes away. If you can get to this point, adhering to a much smaller budget becomes a lot easier as you realize just how unnecessary material things are, not to mention how they have absolutely no effect on your survival or happiness. The key issue is if you can make it that critical amount of time for a month or two to have this new normal set in. But once you do, you will prove to yourself and your hind brain just how pointless and unnecessary the majority of your spending is.

Replacement Drug – Again, the larger aim of this book is to replace your material desires with comradery, friendship, and love for your fellow man. However, humans are not the only thing that can provide purpose, value, and agency in your life. Furthermore, it's not like there's an unlimited supply of quality humans laying around, readily available to become your new family, friends, and loved ones. Ergo, you'll need a substitute until that point in time. Things like picking up a hobby, working out, joining a religion, returning to school, volunteering, getting a second job, meditating, even getting a dog are all healthy things to keep yourself out of the mall and off of Amazon.com. Additionally, as it just so happens, these "substitutes" are extremely valuable in that they are what ultimately makes you a unique and interesting human. A unique and interesting human other humans will want in their lives.

Therapy – Because of the parallels and root origins materialism and conventional addiction share, getting the help of a professional that specializes in addiction cannot hurt. Yes, it might cost you a couple hundred bucks. And yes, having a spending problem presents nowhere near the problems that being a meth addict does. But if it helps cut your spending, getting the insights of an independent, impartial, third party may be well worth your time and money.

Extraneous Limitations – Much like committing yourself to rehab, there are measures you can take that will simply eliminate your ability to spend money. Cutting up your credit cards, placing withdrawal limits on your bank account, the "envelope budgeting method," etc. To this day I still only have a $3,000 limit on my credit card which ensures against any impulsive purchases of cars, motorcycles, or other expensive items, not to mention, thieves. Place similar restrictions on all your purchasing means to simply prevent you from spending more than you have.

<u>Solitary Confinement</u> – My CPA friend employs a very clever strategy. He worked at one of the Big 4 accounting firms, slaving away in a soulless cubicle job, dealing with the mentally taxing politics of being under the employ of one of these ~~arrogant~~ "enviable" firms. One day he had enough, figured for a fraction of the effort he could make thrice the money going it alone, and he now runs his own successful accountancy.

But he faced a problem.

With today's modern internet technology, there was no reason to rent an office. Additionally, he's so efficient, he doesn't need employees and is a one man operation. So even though he was living the American dream - sleeping in till 10AM, doing all of his work in his pajamas, and then maybe going to the bar to meet clients for scotch - he was increasingly miserable. And the reason was the lack of human interaction.

To solve this problem he decided to work as a contractor for three months a year after busy season. This would force him to commute, force him to sit in a cubicle, force him to do mind-numbing work, harshly reminding him as to how fortunate he was to have the self-employment gig he set up for himself. However, it would also allow him to interact with other humans, ending the ennui that was plaguing him at his home office.

The lesson to learn from this is that while humans are the sole cause of all the world's problems and the bane of our existence, the only thing worse than having them around is not having them around at all. Yes, you can't wait to leave your beer-swilling husband for that girls' weekend escape up at that cabin. Yes, you playfully toy with the idea of pushing your nagging wife into a lake and running off to play poker with the guys. And siblings are not siblings unless they are fighting with each other, occasionally drawing blood.

But have you ever gone without humans?

Go on a two week motorcycle ride and you'll soon miss your wife's nitpicking on how you do the laundry.

Jet off to Italy and you'll oddly enough miss your husband's fart jokes and commensurate farting.

And when your kids go off to college, leaving the home forever, very few mothers make it more than 10 minutes before breaking down and crying.

Again, like a funeral, we don't appreciate people until they're gone. And whatever annoying eccentricities that drove us insane about them before, become endearing quirks we cherish and miss about their personalities. But instead of waiting for people to die or leave home for college, why not do what my friend did and put yourself in solitary confinement, fasting from your fellow humans?

This doesn't mean you have be stationed in Iraq for three uninterrupted tours, or pull a Daniel Boone, living in the wilderness for years on end. But purposely cutting yourself off from humans for weeks, even months at a time really puts things in perspective and truly shows you the value of your fellow man. I personally go on months-long motorcycling-hiking adventures in the American west, in part because it's my passion, but also it forces me to appreciate my friends and loved ones back home. My accounting buddy puts himself through the rat-race torture of commutes, cubicles, and corporations, all so he cherishes his self-employment and the friends he has. If you do the same, I can almost guarantee you'll never care about material possessions again, and will gladly take a good conversation with a friend over a designer handbag from New York.

You Will Suffer – It is amazing as to what lengths the human mind will go to avoid pain and suffering. This is only outdone by the Olympian level of mental acrobatics humans will perform to lie to themselves that they should *never suffer pain in their entire lives.* Be it entitlement, the cushy life modern day technology affords us, or simply a gigantic lapse in logic, most people believe their lives should be void of pain. But understand this about life, and especially understand this about improving one's life:

You

Will

Suffer

There is no avoiding pain in life. Merely postponing it into the future where it will accrue interest and grow into an even more insufferable amount of pain. You either accept that pain is part of life and endure it at opportune, beneficial moments, or save it up for so long that it will cripple, break, and bankrupt you in the future.

In short, accept the fact that there's going to be a little bit of pain in "doing without." Which is going to be an infinitesimal fraction of the amount of pain that you'll wreak upon yourself if you inadequately prepare for retirement and outlive your money.

CHAPTER 3
PRINCIPLES

In the perfect world all 240 million American adults will have read this essay, realized that humans are the most important thing in life, and eliminated all desire for material things. This in theory would change the country's financial behaviors overnight to the point that the financial pieces to our retirement puzzle would naturally and effortlessly fall into place. We would cut our budgets across the board by at least 50%, pay off all our debts, save more-than-enough money to adequately fund a full retirement, spend more time with families and loved ones, and thus live much better and happier lives.

But even if we have the most thorough understanding of this new retirement philosophy and fully intend to implement it in our lives, it still helps to have a roadmap or instruction manual as to how to practically do so. And whereas there is certainly no limit to the number of budgets, books, methods, or programs to help cut your spending, I prefer a more overarching, principled approach to specific, restrictive, and literal ones.

Principles of the New Retirement

The reason I do not like budgets is because of the exact same reason I do not like our current retirement system. It assumes everything is under our control. It assumes it is a science. It assumes that there is a finite formula or algorithm that if followed, will always work out in the end. This is simply not true. Medical emergencies, car repairs, deaths, honest (but costly) human mistakes, oopsy babies, cancer, winning the lottery, crashing a car, an unexpected inheritance from a great uncle - there are simply too many variables outside of our control that pop into our lives and render most budgets moot.

Ergo, in the practice of stoicism and acknowledging what we do and do not control, I prefer instead to manage my finances via principles and policies. Rules I simply follow, never break, and if I adhere to them in the long run, financial success and an adequate retirement are all but guaranteed. This isn't to say that setting a personal budget is foolish or has no value, but when it comes to practicality, efficacy, and actual techniques that work, it's infinitely easier following a handful of rules than tracking your finances to the penny.

Minimalism

The overall guiding principle that should govern your future finances should be one of minimalism. This means different things to different people, but it simply means buying only what you need. I've known some minimalists who take it to an extreme, living in communes, only using public transportation, one even squatting in an abandoned house so he doesn't have to pay for rent. You certainly have every right to go and squat in houses, but minimalism does not mean poverty. It simply means before you buy something you ask, "Do I NEED this?"

What you'll find out is that it's pretty easy to determine what you do and do not need. Food, clothing, and shelter are the bare necessities.

But a trap many novice minimalists fall into is tripping over dollars to pick up dimes. i.e. - being cheap for cheap's sake. This can cost you a LOT of money in a very short time, not to mention ruin your life. Buying dirt cheap cars can not only cost you more in repairs, but land you in a hospital when the axle goes out and you crash into a semi. Defending yourself in court can save you some cash up front, but can also land you in prison. And yes, you can use the library's internet for free, but somebody can easily hack your banking, credit card, and social media accounts, stealing your money and identity. So follow the rule of being frugal, not cheap.

Get Rid of Your Stuff

Perhaps one of the best scenes in American cinema is from the movie "American Beauty." A couple is having marital problems. Yet, in a charming and innocent way, the husband tries to rekindle the relationship by seducing his wife in the middle of the day when their child isn't home. Right upon the precipice of wooing her fully, she realizes he's about to spill beer on the couch, and horrifically ruins the moment by saying, "Oh Lester, you're about to spill beer on the couch!"

Frustrated, the husband gets up in disbelief and says, "So what? It's just a couch."

To which his wife painfully defends, "This is a $4,000 sofa, upholstered in Italian silk!"

This enrages Lester, launching him into a tirade that despite it being Italian silk and expensive, it is indeed just a couch, a mere thing, a thing that like all the other things in their house is ruining their relationship and lives.

Nearly everything in your house or apartment is "just a couch." Completely unnecessary and unneeded. And while you should certainly have furniture, appliances, beds and entertainment systems, the truth is those necessities take up a minority of the space. If you were to fully inventory all the things in your house you will find the majority of it is worthless, meaningless crap that is just taking up space.

Clothes you haven't worn or haven't fit into in years.
Books you'll never read again, movies you'll never watch again.
Doilies and trinkets that collect dust and only serve to make cleaning more difficult.
Toys your kids rapidly became bored with, crowding the attic.
Toys your husband never fixes or repairs, preventing you from parking your vehicles in the garage.

The list goes on, but when you calculate it your home is not so much a place to house humans, but is predominantly a storage facility for stuff you don't use or need.

This is true expense of consumerism because whereas it certainly costs a lot to buy all these material things up front, it costs a lot more to house them. And if you were to truly inventory all that is in your house, you'll realize nearly 2/3rds of your square footage is dedicated to storing stuff, which means 2/3rds of your largest expense (rent/mortgage) is utterly wasted.

Therefore, one of the first (and best) things you should do is declutter and eliminate all the unnecessary stuff you have in your house or apartment. Certainly keep mementoes, certainly keep keepsakes, and certainly keep the big screen TV, but ideally each person should be able to fit their entire worldly possessions into a single truck bed. This will not only simplify your life and be a huge psychological relief, but it will allow you to downsize your house or apartment, drastically cutting your single largest living expense.

Eliminate All Debts

The number one thing keeping Americans down is not your boss, "the corporations," "the man," "the system," "the po po," the politicians, or the illuminati.

It is the interest you pay on your self-inflicted debts.

The way it works is that most people cannot afford big ticket items with cash. They are also unwilling to take the time to save up the money

to buy these big ticket items. They want it
NOW. So the solution nearly everyone employs
is debt. This allows people to buy things they
can't afford now, and pay for them later.

But debt comes with a price – interest.

To get people to lend you money you need to
pay these lenders interest. And this would be
fine if you're borrowing $2,000 here or $4,000
there for the occasional unexpected or
emergency expense. But when you borrow

$500,000 for that McMansion just to be in a
good school district,
$75,000 for that Mercedes to impress your co-
workers,
$25,000 on your credit card for clothes, or
$250,000 for that arts degree from that
prestigious New England liberal arts college

the principal amount is so large that the interest
expense you pay becomes the all-consuming
expense in your budget.

This results in you earning the unenviable title of

"debt slave." Your debts are so large that all you can afford to pay is the interest on your debts, and never the debt itself, thus enslaving you to those debts forever. Alas, people no longer buy what they can afford, but what they can finance. They do not buy a house, but a house payment. They do not buy a car, but a car payment. And almost to the penny, Americans will borrow until ALL their income is consumed by interest expense, leaving nothing for retirement, fun, travel, vacationing, or their children.

The solution is simple and two-fold. One, never get into debt in the first place. Because of the compound mathematical nature of interest, it is exponentially harder to get out of debt, than if you just saved up the money over time and paid cash. Be patient, take your time, save your pennies and dimes, and pay cash for all your major purchases. Two, if you're in debt do everything in your power to get out. This typically means cutting your budget, selling your assets, but above all else, working a second or third job to pay off your debts. It may result in a few years of pain and misery, but that's better than the lifetime of misery you will suffer if you never get out from under your debts.

No Future "Non-Investment" Debt

Once debt-free ensure you never take on any non-investment debt ever again. While in the ideal world you would never take on any debt, period, debt can serve to help you financially if it is used for a wise investment. The reason being is that investments provide a rate of return, and if that rate of return is higher than the interest rate you pay on your debts, you can actually make money, perhaps even become rich.

What constitutes an investment, however, is not so clear. People say "education is an investment" or "your house is an investment," but in reality they're not. Your house is NOT an investment because what profits does your house generate? In reality it is a necessary expense that you knowingly and willingly pay because you need lodging. It may go up in price and provide you a capital gain (much like the magically-forever-increasing stock market), but the house as an underlying asset does not generate any cash flow or profits to pay the mortgage and is therefore not an investment.

Education is also increasingly less of an investment and more an expensive hobby. If you major in engineering, computer programming, or attend trade school, the case can be made that the money you invested in your education will generate higher lifetime earnings, and is therefore an investment. But it's laughable to spend $150,000 on worthless degrees such as English, Women's Studies, Communications, and other liberal arts claptrap, yet claim it's an "investment" while you're serving coffee as a barista at $8 an hour. Worse, this "investment" typically cripples young people financially for their entire lives as they never get out from underneath their student loans.

The trick is to make sure you don't make any STUPID investments. For example, during my days in banking, every recently-divorced, middle-aged man going through a midlife crisis wanted to start a sports bar. This along with every middle-aged woman who thought her coffee shop, used clothing store, or trinket shop was her path to riches. In reality the majority of "investments" people make are hobbies they personally want to do, not what the market demands and is willing to pay for. This is why nearly every sports bar goes under, every horse farm goes bankrupt, every restaurant changes hands every three years, and baristas all have humanities degrees. If you're going to invest, INVEST in an asset that generates a profit or a business that produces something people are willing to pay for. Not some stupid idealistic dream that will turn into a financial nightmare.

Pay Cash for Cars

Though thoroughly covered under the aforementioned debt-avoiding principles, it's worth reiterating the importance of avoiding debt, especially when it comes to cars. Because while you might own a house or two in your entire lifetime, you will likely purchase over a dozen cars. With the average price of a car going for $33,600, this translates into about $403,000 in lifetime car purchases, the equivalent to a very nice house. When you throw in interest expense (as 85% of people either lease or finance their cars) the figure is closer to $500,000, the average amount needed today to retire.

The majority of this expense is simply unnecessary. One, insist on only paying cash for cars. This will avoid incurring any interest expense that will further enslave you to your debt. Second, never buy new. With today's automotive technology, you can find a perfectly good used car with low mileage for a quarter of the price new. Again, you can have transportation and an adequately-funded retirement, or prestigious vanity and no retirement at all. Used cars bought with cash afford you the former.

Do Not Legally Entwine Yourself with People Who Have Financial Problems

If you put in the pain, work, toil and effort to become debt-free, that is a huge and very rare achievement. You rightly deserve the life of serenity, peace, and calm that comes with it. But all that hard work can be undone if you legally tether yourself to those who are fiscally irresponsible and reckless. Be it marriage, co-habitation (in some states), business partnerships, even lending people money, becoming financially and legally intertwined with people who have financial problems can undo all your hard work and financial effort. A spouse with a spending problem. Your old high school buddy who wants you to help him finance a sports bar. Even your children who want you to co-sign their loans so they can get a Doctorate in Literature. All these people, loved ones or not, can torpedo your otherwise healthy finances.

Therefore, do not go through all the work, toil, and suffering to set yourself financially free only to re-enslave yourself to other people's bad debts. Simply refuse any financial, business, or personal dealings with people who have poor finances, unsupportable debts, and bad financial habits.

Buy Only as Much House as You Need

Since lodging is the single largest expense in most people's lives, ensuring you only have what is absolutely necessary, and not a square foot more, will go a long way in shoring up your personal finances. Be it:

- The student debt addled 20 something who just "has to" live in the coolest (and most expensive) part of town
- The dude bro, "$30,000-Dollarnaire" who needs his "pimpin'" downtown condo
- Or the perfect suburbanite "power couple" who need to own the most luxurious five-bedroom house in the development (though having zero kids)

ALL of them are guaranteed to have unrecoverable financial problems in the future.

Make sure this isn't you.

When looking for housing spend the time to fully analyze your housing options to find the one that works best for you. You may want to move into the city to cut your commute time. You may want to move out to farm country because you can work from home. Property taxes could be so egregious it's better to rent a house than to buy. And moving across the street could land your kids in a much better school district. The truth is there are no universal rules or principles when it comes to housing because real estate is highly variable depending upon location, taxation, state law, city law, property taxes, the local housing market, and your own personal situation. So spend the hours, even days if necessary thoroughly researching your local housing market. It can be the difference between having a house paid off when you're 35 or being 60 and looking to get approved for Section 8 housing.

"The Steve Jobs is Dead Principle"

The two most famous celebrities to come out of Silicon Valley are Bill Gates and Steve Jobs. Both were billionaires before 40. Both were titans in their industry. Both developed technologies that revolutionized the world. And both are household names.

About the only difference is that Bill Gates is alive and Steve Jobs is dead.

Steve Jobs' early demise, however, teaches us a very valuable lesson, and that lesson is that time is more important than money.

Bill Gates, for example, in spite of his billions, is statistically likely to die in 18 years when he turns 79. He could live longer, he could die sooner, but the point is he's no different than any other man, he's just richer. And that means unless you have a pre-existing medical condition, you, me, and every other person out there have the exact same amount of time on this planet as Bill. The question is how do you want to spend it?

While everybody pursues wealth and wants to become rich, the truth is if it doesn't result in extended life expectancy, then why pursue it? As long as you have food, clothing, shelter, and don't live in abject poverty, you will have the exact same life expectancy as Bill Gates. Matter of fact, it behooves a very interesting question of Bill. Would he not have been better off spending more time with Melinda instead of all that time founding and running Microsoft? All those billions of dollars doesn't grant you any extra years of life over a guy who makes $40,000 a year and works half as much, so why work so hard?

All of this is doubly reinforced with Steve Jobs.

Steve Jobs was just as rich, but tragically died at 56. What good did all that money do him? A long life on this planet just wasn't in the cards for him, and though he left an amazing legacy for the world to know, he may have very well gladly traded it all in to spend a higher percentage of those short 56 years with family and loved ones.

This is the point of "The Steve Jobs is Dead Principle." That you should work to live, not live to work. While a career is absolutely necessary to put food on the table and a roof over your head, too many people put their career above loved ones, even making it what defines them in life. People actually place more value on "closing the sale" or "getting the contract" than fishing with their son or helping a friend fix a car. Worse, people have more pride in titles like "investment banker" or "professor" than they do "wife," "father," "friend" or "buddy." In reality your career is a necessary evil that competes against the humans in your life for your finite and precious time. To the millisecond, every second you spend at work is one less second you spend in life. Work is your enemy, not your friend. Make sure it works for you.

No Commute

Much like "Always Pay Cash for Cars" is a reinforcement of the "No Non-Investment Debt Principle," refusing to commute is a reinforcement of the "Steve Jobs is Dead Principle." You simply do not have the life expectancy to waste 12% of your adult waking life in traffic. And society can certainly do without all the damaging secondary effects commutes wreak upon it. Stress, divorce, ill-reared children, health problems, mental problems, and shortened life expectancies, all of it is an unacceptable proposition from commutes.

Eliminate, or at least shorten commutes to the maximum extent possible in life. Even if it costs more, rent a place where you can walk to work. If you're not too sure about the stability of your job, spring the extra bucks on a month-to-month lease. If you're about to enter college, study a subject that allows you to work from home (computer programming, IT, etc.). And if you can manage it, insist on telecommuting. The technology exists today that nearly all white collar/non-trade work can be done from home. And while a lot of traditional, outdated corporate culture insists you unnecessarily commute to an office, make it a policy you simply do not commute. A lot of people may make the case "well we can't all work from home," which is true. Just have the self-respect to make sure you're one of the lucky few who does.

Entrepreneurship

Entrepreneurship is a further extension of "The Steve Jobs is Dead Principle." For while the goal is to make your job "work for you," no profession works for you better than being self-employed. You answer to no one, you don't deal with office politics, you don't have a commute (unless you want one), the profits are theoretically unlimited, but above all else it's entirely flexible and conducive to living life.

There is, however, one additional advantage to entrepreneurship. It can play a major role in your retirement.

While the bond and stock markets only provide 2% yields to investors today, if you choose the right entrepreneurial endeavor you can likely earn a lot more. For example, not to be crass, but I run a company called "Asshole Consulting." And I face a choice. I can either invest my money in an IRA where I'll earn the standard market rate of 2%, or I can spend money on advertising which has historically provided around a 20% rate of return. Another author friend of mine can invest in his 401k at work, or spend money advertising his books which provides him an estimated 40% rate of return. And my accounting buddy can invest in a Roth IRA if he wants, but why would he when he can hire a staff accountant and increase his profits by 50%? The point is that if you pick the right business, entrepreneurship can not only provide you a living, but provide for your retirement as well.

Save for Retirement

You'll notice if you practice all the principles mentioned above you'll likely have a lot of money left over every month. And if you eliminate all your debts, you'll definitely have a lot of money left over every month. But remember, the whole point of this essay is to have a successful retirement. **DON'T FORGET TO INVEST IT.**

Certainly go on trips, spend time with friends, eat good food, and experience all this world has to offer, but not until you FIRST squirrel away some money for retirement. Matter of fact, the first thing you should do after paying all essential expenses is throw a predetermined amount into your IRA, 401k, or (if going the entrepreneurial route) your business. Again, this will not guarantee that the stock market won't crash or your business won't fail, but you are guaranteed to have a miserable old age if you fail to save for retirement.

<u>Never Retire</u>

While our minds' perception of retirement are pictures of sunny Florida beaches, white hats, boats, glasses of wine, svelte aged-wives, and Viagra commercials, the reality of retirement is much different.

Retirement is death.

At first you may laugh, finding the claim a bit radical, but it becomes very somber when you look at depression and suicide rates post retirement. Initially after retirement most people enjoy a bump in their mental and physical health, finally freed from work, ne'er to punch a time clock again. But after an initial honeymoon period the reality of retirement sets in. And you soon realize you've served your purpose in life and the world no longer needs you. You are literally just killing time.

This triggers an existential crisis which is only

worsened by several other factors. One, your entire brain was conditioned and programmed for 50 years to work. And though consciously you may have detested work, it was a reliable and constant variable in your life that you unconsciously grew accustomed (and ultimately addicted) to. The bus route you drove every day, the Monday morning ribbing you'd give your co-workers, the shop talk you'd have in the break room, that regular routine played a large role in your life by the simple fact it consumed such a large percentage of it. That large part of your life is now gone.

Two, the human brain is not genetically programmed to retire. The vast majority of humans simply worked until they died. And while that may sound tragic, it's what two million years of evolution has programmed us to do. In other words, retirement is not natural and will not feel natural to most people. At best this will cause some mental discomfort, at worse it will add to your depression.

Closely related, three, most people derive some kind of life purpose, reason, and agency through their work. Ask a person to tell them about themselves and they'll likely lead off with what their profession is. But now with that profession gone, precisely who are you and what value do you bring to this world? Again, you could have very well worked up millions of dollars' worth of value for society, more than earning your right to retire. But your hindbrain does not care. For most people if they're not producing something or doing something, life quickly loses meaning and purpose.

Finally, novelty. No matter how many boats you sail, chardonnays you drink, beaches you bum on, all with an amazingly svelte 63 year old Ann Margaret-esque wife, it will get boring. This is a simple, though unfortunate law of economics. Everything inevitably loses its value, including retirement. Soon you'll be sick of fishing every morning even though that was your retirement dream. You'll be sick of having your morning espresso with the ladies' bridge club even though you looked forward to it on weekends back home. And even that perfect view of those pristine white beaches you paid $3.5 million to buy that condo on will lose its appeal.

In short, retirement is not a final solution or answer to any of life's problems, but a mere stage in life that presents its own problem, namely what do you do now? And sadly, there is no answer or solution to that problem.

Alas, it is no shock that after retirement your chances for being diagnosed with depression increases by 40%. Worse, your chances for being diagnosed with a medical condition increases by 60% (compared to a non-retired peer group). And even worse than that, if you're male suicide rate triples after age 65 (though it is duly noted many men opt for suicide if diagnosed with a terminally ill disease). Retirement is not going to be the problem-free utopian life pictured in Viagra commercials. It is going to be a huge mental and philosophical challenge we will all get to face as we stare down the barrel of our own mortality and reason for being. But there is a solution that solves nearly all these problems, not to mention drastically improves our retirement finances.

Don't retire.

This doesn't mean to keep working the job you hate and couldn't wait to retire from for the past 40 years. But it does mean to find some job, ANY job that gives you point and purpose in life, a reason to get up in the morning, people to interact with, and a little bit of money on the side. If you've adequately saved for retirement, pay won't be an issue, allowing you to work more enjoyable jobs. You also won't have to tolerate abuse or the slightest bit of lip from co-workers or bosses because you don't need the money. And if you're REALLY smart, you'll have used the past 40 years to set up a profitable entrepreneurial venture you thoroughly enjoy pursuing as it's your passion. But whatever you do, do not so poorly plan or anticipate your retirement that your best option is to waste your social security check and last days in life on slot machines in a casino.

CHAPTER 4
IMPLEMENTATION

Numbers

The aforementioned principles and philosophies are all very nice and, if followed, will almost guarantee you'll save up enough for a successful retirement. But we still need to run some numbers in order to establish our retirement savings goals, measure our progress towards reaching them, as well as give us some guidelines as to what our budget should look like today, as well as during retirement.

To get the most accurate numbers we need to be both conservative and thorough, ensuring we do not miss any expenses we'd likely incur. And while it may seem a bit overkill there is no better template that achieves this than Microsoft Excel's highly detailed personal budget template (https://www.smartsheet.com/file/personal-budget-templatev20.xlsx).

Expenses from Microsoft's Personal Budget Template

HOME
Mortgage/Rent
Home/Rental Insurance
Electricity
Gas/Oil
Water/Sewer/Trash
Phone
Cable/Satellite
Internet
Furnishing/Appliances
Lawn/Garden
Maintenance/Improvements
Other

TRANSPORTATION
Car payments
Auto Insurance
Fuel
Public Transportation
Repairs/Maintenance
Registration/License

DAILY LIVING

Groceries
Child care
Dining out
Clothing
Cleaning
Salon/Barber
Pet Supplies

ENTERTAINMENT
Video/DVD/Movies
Concerts/Plays
Sports
Outdoor Recreation

HEALTH
Health Insurance
Gym membership
Doctors/Dentist visits
Medicine/Prescriptions
Veterinarian
Life Insurance

VACATION/HOLIDAY
Airfare
Accommodations
Food

Souvenirs
Pet Boarding
Rental car

From this we should be able to parse out a
personal budget that works for the Average Joe.
But who is "Average Joe?" No two people are
the same and therefore no two people will have
the same budget. Some people have kids, others
are childless. Some people have lengthy
commutes, others work from home. Some
people live in expensive cities, others live in
cheap rural farmlands. Therefore, for the sake
of analysis we are going to assume Average Joe is
a truly average individual. He lives in
Averageville, AV, has an average commute, has
average tastes, and lives an average life.
However, we are also going to assume he is
childless and practices the principles of
minimalism mentioned above. This will allow us
to focus only on what one individual needs to
save for retirement, as well as allow us to
discover what the absolute minimum budget is
for one person to successfully live and retire.
This isn't to say you will go without luxuries
such as eating out, vacations, and movies, but it

will serve as a base model budget by which we can work from and build upon.

Average Joe's Minimalist Budget

Mortgage/Rent	$700
Electric	$30
Gas	$30
Phone	$40
Internet	$40
Auto Insurance	$100
Fuel	$100
Auto Repairs	$50
Groceries	$150
Health Insurance	$100
Dentist	$50
Total Monthly Expenses	$1,390

Though there is certainly room for debate, the above budget highlights something very important and that is just how little an individual needs to survive. While everybody is obsessed about making six figures, driving German imports, and ordering $500 bottle service in Vegas, Average Joe manages to live off of $1,390 a month, or $16,700 per year. This right here proves that you can live off of very little, a mere $8.18 per hour. It may not be a fun life, it may not be an enjoyable life, but to just survive in America one really only needs to make $8.18 per hour.

Thankfully, Average Joe makes a lot more than that as the real median income in the US is $30,500, a full $13,800 more than what he needs. Naturally, with taxes he does not get to keep all $13,800, but his minimalism serves him well again because at that low income tax bracket he only pays an estimated $1000 in tax (after tax credits, standard deductions, etc.). This leaves $12,800 in disposable income for him to spend on whatever he wants. The question is does that afford him enough money to pay for retirement?

And the answer is a resounding yes.

Assuming Average Joe is 30, has 35 years until he retires, throws all of the $12,800 into his retirement account, and earns 6% a year on his investments, he will have $1,426,000 saved up.

RETIREMENT AMOUNT CALCULATOR	
Current Age	30
Current Amount in Your Fund	$0
Expected Retirement Age	65
Expected Rate of Return	6%
Annual Amount to Calculate Fund Balance at Retirement	$12,800
Total Amount Saved by 65	**$1,426,365**

This is of course 35 years into the future and that number will be distorted by inflation. But if we adjust for a 2.5% annual inflation rate that translates into $601,000 today, $100,000 more than the standard rule-of-thumb $500,000 people need to retire today.

But here is an interesting question. Does Average Joe really need that magical $500,000 to retire?

While he is Average Joe, he is not average in the fact he is a minimalist and places more value on spending time with friends than spending his money on things. That $500,000 number assumes you're the typical American, loaded to the hilt with debt, blowing your money on things, and still trying to impress your fellow neighborhood soccer moms with your newly leased Range Rover. What does MINIMALIST

Average Joe really need to retire?

Well a lot less than his Range Rover-driving soccer mom counterpart.

First, while the average American will spend $40,000 a year to survive during retirement, Minimalist Average Joe never needed that much to live on in the first place. He was perfectly capable getting by on $17,000. This immediately cuts the amount he needs to retire (in today's dollars) by more than half to $230,000.

RETIREMENT CALCULATOR - HOW MUCH TO RETIRE	
Annual Income Required (today's dollars)	$17,000
Number of Years to Retirement	35
Number of Years Required After Retirement	25
Annual Inflation	0%
Annual Return on Your Investments	6%
Amount Needed for Retirement	$230,357

Second, unlike the average American, Minimalist Average Joe will likely have his house paid off in full by the time he retires. He'll still have to pay property taxes and insurance on his property, but the lack of a mortgage payment will significantly cut his required budget from about $17,000 to $12,000. This in turn will further cut the amount he needs for retirement from $230,000 to a paltry $163,000. In all technicality, Joe will save up that amount by the time he's 43 and his investments do not even need to grow (beyond the rate of inflation).

RETIREMENT CALCULATOR - HOW MUCH TO RETIRE	
Annual Income Required (today's dollars)	$12,000
Number of Years to Retirement	35
Number of Years Required After Retirement	25
Annual Inflation	0%
Annual Return on Your Investments	6%
Amount Needed for Retirement	$162,604

Third, none of this is considering the possibility that Average Joe might collect a social security check. Even if the worst predictions of social security come true and social security only pays out a fraction of what Joe is due, it still makes an already easy financial situation easier. But assuming social security is still around when Joe retires and is not whittled away by inflation, Joe can expect to receive $1,340 monthly in social security (in 2016 dollars). In other words, Average Joe doesn't even have to save for retirement because social security will more than cover his incredibly frugal lifestyle.

While this is all very impressive, the honest truth is that nobody would want to live Minimalist Average Joe's life. He has no fun, never travels, doesn't kiss any girls, and though I do know people who live perfectly happy lives spending even LESS than Minimalist Average Joe, the vast majority of us would be absolutely miserable. But the theoretical retirement scenario we ran with Minimalist Average Joe was not meant to be a recommendation, but a demonstration of feasibility and just how little you need to save for retirement. You do NOT need $500,000 in 2016 dollars to save for retirement. You do NOT need to make the much-touted "six figures" to enjoy life. You just need to put humans first in your life, and spend only what you need.

Still, for practicality's sake, a much more realistic scenario should be run for the benefit of the average American and to give us a benchmark to go by. This would include adding some money to the budget for fun, travel, eating out, and other luxuries (budget below).

Average Joe's Normal Monthly Budget

Mortgage/Rent	900
Electricity	35
Gas/Oil	35
Phone	40
Internet	40
Furnishing/Appliances	20
Maintenance/Improvements	25
Auto Insurance	100
Fuel	100
Repairs/Maintenance	40
Registration/License	10
Groceries	200
Dining out	200
Video/DVD/Movies	20
Concerts/Plays	25
Recreation	20
Health Insurance	100
Gym membership	25
Doctors/Dentist visits	50
Airfare	50
Accommodations	10
Food	20

Rental car	10
Total Expense	$2,075

It would also include an annual income closer to $40,000 as the $30,500 figure includes teenagers, part-time workers, and entry level employees which understate people's income. And if the last principle of never retiring is to be followed, your average American would conservatively only need to save for 20 years of post-retirement life as opposed to 25. When we run these figures a normal, healthy, balanced life, replete with a fully-funded retirement is perfectly within reach of your average, everyday American.

With monthly expenditures of $2,075, but an estimated take home pay of $2,933, the average American can contribute $10,300 annually to their retirement accounts. Over the course of 40 years at a 6% rate of return, you can expect to have just under $1.594 million in your retirement accounts, or $594,000 in today's dollars.

RETIREMENT AMOUNT CALCULATOR	
Current Age	30
Current Amount in Your Fund	$0
Expected Retirement Age	70
Expected Rate of Return	6%
Annual Amount to Calculate Fund Balance at Retirement	$10,300
Total Amount Saved by 70	**$1,594,048**

However, this $594,000 would be unnecessary because if you were to keep up your frugal spending habits, pay off your mortgage, and work into your retirement, you are likely only going to need a third of that to survive retirement.

RETIREMENT CALCULATOR - HOW MUCH TO RETIRE	
Annual Income Required (today's dollars)	$17,700
Number of Years to Retirement	40
Number of Years Required After Retirement	20
Annual Inflation	0%
Annual Return on Your Investments	6%
Amount Needed for Retirement	$215,198

This provides a huge cushion for error when it comes to budgeting and financial planning. But more importantly it practically compels you to occasionally spring for some of the finer things in life. Not to the point that it threatens your finances, but again, it reiterates just what you can afford if you purge yourself of all the worthless material things in your life.

In the end remember these numbers are theoretical. They are mere financial projections and forecasts highly dependent upon the individual, their tastes and preferences, and their financial behaviors. And we haven't even discussed issues such as the tax deductibility of IRA contributions, contribution limits, 401k matching, inflation or the whims of the market. But what we have mathematically proven here is how much simpler, easier, and feasible retirement can be if we simply swap out material things for engaging conversation with the people in our lives.

There's just one final problem.

The Longest Road

While this entire essay is predicated upon placing humans first in your life and living your life for them, the sad truth is that most humans are worthless. Not in a cute sense like your tea-cup dog is a "worthless" dog, incapable of fetching or hunting, but worthless in the literal sense in that they offer absolutely nothing of value to you or society. We may like to think otherwise or even take umbrage to such a pessimistic view of humanity, but take a realistic, unbiased look at all the humans in your life and you'll see it does not paint a pretty picture of humanity.

First, you have people who are just out right evil, who make great Saturday morning cartoon villains. War-mongers, criminals, murderers, slave-traders, rapists, pedophiles, dictators, and terrorists. Inflicting death and misery upon others seem to be the only things that drive them, but these are more statistically-odd historical figures than rank and file everyday people who are in your life.

Unfortunately, second, there are rank and file everyday evil people in your life. Sadistic bosses. Vindictive co-workers. Abusive exes. Absent parents. Psychopathic bullies. Cheating spouses. Charlatan lawyers. Lying politicians. Biased journalists. Worthless professors. Marketing executives. Professional activists.

Sanctimonious hipsters. All of these people, at their core, are self-serving, lazy people who do not view you as a sentient, conscious human being, deserving of respect and equal treatment, but as a thing, a mere tool to advance their own aims, live off of, and perhaps even unleash abuse upon to make them feel better. And sadly they are not statistical oddities. They number in the billions on this planet and arguably account for half the people you know and have to deal with every day.

Third, what people do remain may not be evil, but damn if they aren't the most boring, lazy, conformist, common group of sheeple that ever grazed the Earth. Women who actually read those tabloids in the grocery checkout lane. Men who hork down wings and light beer at the bar as they get emotionally depressed if "their team" doesn't win the game. The legions of youth who'd rather play video games than kiss a girl. And the uninteresting masses who watch reality TV shows or whatever slop is being served on the boobtube today. They may not be evil, but they are certainly not going to be the humans who give you point, purpose, and inspiration to live.

And if this still doesn't convince you, fourth, the people who presumably love you. Most notably your spouse. Out of all the people in the world who you're supposed to love the most, and who should love you the most in return, it should be your spouse. But if you look at the state of marriage, THE pinnacle relationship that should define and give your life purpose above all others, it is laughably tragic and sad.

Half of marriages end in divorce, while the other half is completely miserable. Both husbands and wives let themselves go physically, becoming fat, obese, and physically revolting slobs. Neither do anything to become a more interesting and engaging person. And instead of being the reason people get up in the morning, spouses more often than not tend to become the bane of the other's existence. We all like to point at that cute couple who are truly in love, celebrating their 60th wedding anniversary, as the ole man romantically pinches his wife in the ass, leaving us to speculate whether they're still having sex. But the truth is we just plain don't want to put the effort or work into it, no matter how much we claim we'd like to have that.

This, above all else, highlights the largest problem in pursuing a life where humans are at its center, and the retirement philosophy that happens to come with it – good, quality, engaging people are incredibly rare. If you stop and think about it, out of the SEVEN BILLION people on the planet, how many do you have in your close, personal life that you truly love? How many people do you choose to spend your precious and finite time on this planet with? And out of those precious few, how many do you actually like? It's not until you realize just how few people there are on this planet that aren't evil, aren't boring, have interesting personalities, while at the same time want to spend their time with you, will you truly appreciate their existence in your life. But when you do, that's the point in life where you truly appreciate what you have and who you have in your life. That's the point in life where you can truly be happy. That's the point in life where you're the world's richest person because you have everything you could ever need.

That's also the point in life when they inevitably go away.

Attrition

Fight it all you want, there is an unstoppable force that will take away those precious few humans who give you point and purpose in life. And while you might be tempted to guess this unstoppable force is death, it is quite the opposite.

It's life.

Look back in your life and you will likely find a point where you were surrounded by friends, colleagues, loved ones, and comrades. It could be your fraternity or sorority days where you and your friends enjoyed some of the greatest times together. It could be the military where you and your brothers endured, but survived a hellish existence in the Middle East. The police department where you patrolled a beat with a score of other cops for decades. Or just the office where you actually put in your 35 years to get that watch. It doesn't matter whether the place was enjoyable or not, either taking shots in college or getting shot at in Iraq, but the time you spent together combined with the experiences you shared forged you a surrogate family. A group of friends whose company you thoroughly enjoyed and gave your life meaning and purpose. You just couldn't think of a group of people you'd rather spend time with than these cherished souls.

But what happens after you graduate?
Or the war is over?
Or you retire from the force?

No matter how strong the bonds, the surrogate family disintegrates and goes away.

This is not malicious or intended, but merely the consequences of living. Whatever friends and loved ones you have are inevitably pulled away by the normal forces of life. When you graduate from college you're supposed to pursue your career, even if that means in another state. When you leave the military you're supposed to pursue a civilian life, even if the people who mean the most to you are back in Mosul. And when you retire from work you're supposed to move to Florida, even if your entire social network is at the office. But what's sad is even if you realize the value of having these people in your life, even if you know to cherish these people, you're powerless to do anything about it. Either because there's no reason to stay (college and wars do end) or because people choose to go down a different path (how do you prevent your best friends from retiring to Florida or starting a family in Des Moines?).

This puts even more focus and value on the people who are statistically likely to be in your life for the long run. Most notably your family. It is not coincidence your spouse and children are the most important people in your life because life inevitably pulls everyone else away in their own direction, usually families of their own. But while this puts the pinnacle level of importance on choosing the right spouse and (if you choose to) raising quality, interesting children, even your family will inevitably disband. Ideally, because your children grow up and pursue their own lives, or forcibly and destructively through the wonderful wonders of divorce. What this means is that humans, no matter how dear to you, are not constant variables in life you can take for granted. They are always coming and going. And this highlights the real hurdle and challenge of this new retirement program – you must constantly be on the hunt for new and interesting people in your life.

If there is a drawback to this new retirement system, this is it. And your entire retirement success depends on how you deal with this drawback. Do you try a 44th time to get your friend to get permission from his fiancée to grab a beer with you, even though the past 43 times failed miserably (true story)? Do you pull teeth asking your girlfriend to grab dinner, knowing full well she'll be "too tired," opting to waste her life "staying in." Do you painfully pine to get back together with your ex, all in the vain hopes of rebuilding that nuclear family you once had? Or do you accept the reality of the situation, stoically acknowledge what you do and do not control, and go back out into the world to find some new people who are willing to be a part of your life?

The truth is you'll waste more energy trying to keep people in your life than you will finding new ones. And if you don't realize this you will condemn yourself to a life of misery, failure, depression, perhaps even returning to a life of materialism, vice, and booze, simply because it's an easy and immediate fix. The trick is one of acceptance, moving on, and fully appreciating the daunting task that lies ahead of you. It is a full-time job to go and seek out new and interesting people who are going to make your life worth living. And you don't have a choice lest you want the typical American life filled with cold, material things and not loving, interactive people. You need to go find friends, you need to find colleagues, you need to find fellow souls, with the full and complete understanding that nearly all of them will someday leave and never be seen again. But no matter how much you like them, no matter how much you love them, don't be sad when they go, either because of life or death. Just be happy you got to converse with them while they were there. That is the secret to a successful retirement.

THE END

ADDENDUM AND RESOURCES

The intent of this essay was to provide a new philosophy that would drastically lessen the amount of money people would need to retire, making retirement a reality for all people. However, the actual process of saving for retirement, setting up retirement accounts, choosing a broker, contributing to retirement plans, etc., is a completely different topic, deserving of its own book. Conveniently enough, there are already scores of books written on this topic, but to provide you with an introductory education on the subject I've compiled the following resources below that I hope provides you a starting point and proves useful as well.

"Retirement Planning in 10 Minutes"

I have put together a video that provides a brief overview of retirement planning. I would recommend starting here as it will provide a bird's eye view of what you need to do for retirement, as well as put everything else into context. You can find it on my YouTube channel using the link below (or by searching "Retirement Planning in 10 Minutes"):

https://www.youtube.com/watch?v=TfpTwnGmGig

Retirement Calculators

One of the first things you'll need to do is calculate how much you'll need for retirement. In the past this required some rather bothersome mathematics, but now there are dozens of retirement calculators online that does this for you. There are pros and cons to all of them, but I prefer the following two:

<u>Bloomberg's Retirement Calculator</u>
https://www.bloomberg.com/personal-finance/calculators/retirement/

<u>Bankrate's "How Much to Retire Calculator"</u>
http://www.bankrate.com/calculators/retirement/retirement-calculator.aspx

These two calculators will allow you to calculate the two numbers that will set the tone for the rest of your retirement:

1. How much you need to retire
2. How much you'll need to save each year to reach that amount

"Stocks, Bonds, Investing: Oh My!"

If you are looking for something a bit more thorough than online calculators, videos, or books, you may be interested in an online class I teach titled "Stocks, Bonds, Investing: Oh My!" In full disclosure, yes, I profit from people taking this class. And in additional full disclosure, yes, I fully intend to make as much money as possible! Still, my personal financial interests aside, it is a much more thorough (and expensive) option to learn the basics of 401k's, IRA's, retirement planning, the stock market, trading, etc. You can find it here:

https://www.ed2go.com/online-courses/stocks-bonds-and-investing-oh-my

"Bachelor Pad Economics"

A much cheaper option to the class would be my book "Bachelor Pad Economics." Though written for men and addressing all financial aspects of life (not just retirement), the laws of finance and economics are universal for all people, and this book would be beneficial to anyone who would read it. Though I must warn you it is a book *written for men.* Not women. It includes crass language, locker room talk, and blunt advice on the pursuit of the fairer sex that I'm sure not everybody would approve of. Still, because of its direct nature I believe it would be of immense benefit to everybody...especially women who dare to be bold enough to read it! You can find it on Amazon.com.

Podcasts/YouTube Tutorials/Internet Searching

While I'm a big fan of structured education, I'm an even bigger fan of self-teaching. And while books, classes, and seminars will help, there is so much information on the internet for free that you should have no problem educating yourself via the consumption of online tutorials, articles, podcasts, and videos. It may take a significantly longer time to seek out the information you need, but if you have a minimal budget (or you just don't like spending money) a solid weekend dedicated towards researching retirement on the internet should provide you a more-than-adequate education on the processes and procedures in setting up an IRA account and/or contributing to your 401k plan.

VISIT AARON'S VARIOUS SITES

Books:
http://www.amazon.com/Aaron-Clarey/e/B00J1ZC350/

Podcast:
https://soundcloud.com/aaron-clarey/

Blog:
http://captaincapitalism.blogspot.com

Consulting:
http://www.assholeconsulting.com

Twitter:
https://twitter.com/aaron_clarey

Praxey:
http://www.praxey.com/home/user/assholeconsulting

OTHER BOOKS BY AARON

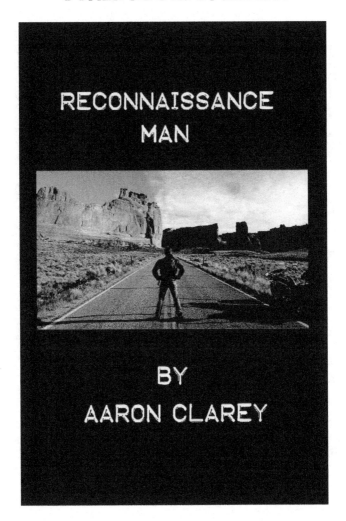

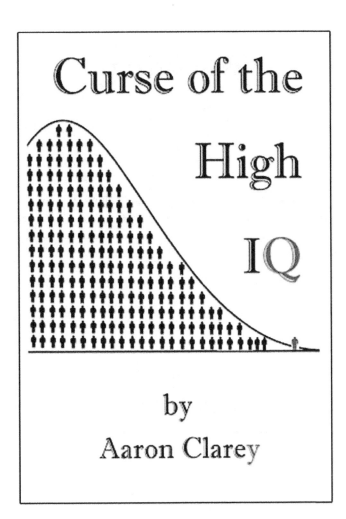

Curse of the

High

IQ

by

Aaron Clarey

Worthless

AMENTIBUS

The Young Person's Indispensable Guide to Choosing the Right Major

By

Aaron Clarey